# BE INSPIRED!

*...win from within.*

**GEORGE O. EMETUCHE**

Copyright © 2019 by George O.Emetuche



Published by The Selling Champion Consulting Limited
51/52 Ijaiye Road,
Ogba- Ikeja
Lagos, Nigeria
234-7060559429, 08186083133
www.thesellingchampionconsulting.com
www.nigeriasalesconference.com
Email:sales@thesellingchampionconsulting.com
george.emetuche@thesellingchampionconsulting.com
sales@nigeriasalesconference.com

ISBN 978-978-56290-8-8

# Dedication

I dedicate this book to everyone who is doing his best to reach his goals.

I dedicate this book to everyone who is fighting the good fight.

# CONTENTS

# ACKNOWLEGEMENTS

I thank God for giving me the ability to invent inspiring thoughts in print. *Be Inspired* is Served!

I appreciate everyone who contributed in one way or the other to what I have become.

To my beautiful wife Maureen, and my adoring Children, Giovanni and Darren, I thank you for your encouragements that made me conclude this book in two weeks.

Be Inspired! You have just picked a book that will stimulate your day. This book *Be Inspired* will unleash the hidden treasures deposited in you.

One of the goals of this book is to motivate you to achieve your objectives in life. In the course of my career as a bestselling author, certified trainer, speaker and sales and marketing consultant, I have met a lot of people in diverse industries. My experience in my career and personal life has taught me that folks become what they think, believe and work on. My experience in my professional life of twenty-two years has also taught me that the more you inspire yourself to win, the more you overcome your challenges; and the more you win. This is what I learned in the school of life.

You are the best gift to your world. It's time to prove your worth. It's time to unleash your value. The world is waiting to have a feel of you. This is your time to shine. This is the time to prove you are unique. But you must take action if you really want to make a difference. You must do something unique if you want to standout. You can't be an outstanding individual by wishing alone. You become the best by taking action. You desire what you want to be, and do the work aspects that will make it come to reality. You must take actions to create the world you desire. Actions beget results.

> *You must take actions to create the world you desire. Actions beget results.*

You must wake up daily and inspire yourself to conquer your world. You are your number one fan. Everyone is waiting for you to inspire yourself first. People will follow you if you *follow* yourself first. People will believe you if you believe yourself. You must conquer yourself. You must win the battle within. You cannot overcome the challenges in your world if you have not conquered the man within. You must win from within by believing in yourself.

> *You must sit down and settle on your destination before you begin the journey of life.*

Life is a journey and we all decide our destinations. You must sit down and settle on your destination before you begin the journey of life. You must make up your mind on the path you want to take. You can't be inspired on nothing. You get inspired on something. The inspiration that will drive your day must be rooted on a firm substance. This means that you must get ready to work if you truly want to stir yourself to win.

Greatness is not attained by imagination only. Prominence is a function of thinking and working. You do the two. This is my philosophy. This is what I promote. You imagine greatness and work it out. You must walk the talk. Attaining greater heights in life is a function of Desire, Action and Faith. I call it, DAF. These three should be in place in order to succeed in life. It follows thus: You must have the desire to succeed, followed by doing the things required to succeed; then believe! You must believe in your dreams. This is not a choice but a necessity. Believing in your dreams is a defined path to Success. This is how to inspire yourself to win.

The presentation style of this book is simple. This book is written for everyone; no matter your status in life. The book will take you to an interesting journey. The thoughts in this book are things you can resonate with. They are thoughts you can feel. They are nuggets that will bring out the champion in you.

I recommend that you read this book at least four times every year to internalize the valuable message in the book. I also recommend that you get copies for your friends. This book is surely a priceless gift. The nuggets herein are practical; they are tasted path to success. I recommend that you apply them.

This is your time. Take it!

Here is the synopsis of this book:

## NUGGET ONE: FIRST THINGS FIRST

This nugget encourages you to start the right way. Successful life follows a defined order. The man on a journey must define how he will embark on the journey. He does the first things first. He designs the way to go and how to get there.

Every airplane takes off from an airport. Every great work begins with a good plan. Doing the right things at the right time is the way of successful people. You must be orderly. You must do first things first if you truly want to be successful. Success doesn't happen by accident. Successful life is planned for. You plan and work for it.

## NUGGET TWO: SHARPEN THE AXE

The second nugget tells the reader to get prepared before taking the journey. The concept of sharpening the axe is relevant in any life endeavour. If you want the axe to do more work, you need to sharpen it now. If you want to get more things done in life, you must begin now to develop yourself in the areas that will help you achieve your goals. There's no better counsel than this!

## NUGGET THREE: YOU DETERMINE THE DIRECTION

The third nugget of this book reminds the reader that he or she has the responsibility to determine the direction of the journey. Many dreams never saw the light of the day because the dreamers lacked the abilities to determine the right directions. They just got stuck on the way and allowed their dreams to die! This is not good news. You must wake up if you want your dreams to come true. You must keep your dreams alive. You must work your way to the top. You must show self-leadership and belief in self. The way to the top is available for individuals who know exactly how to locate and use the ladder that will take them to the top.

## NUGGET FOUR: INSPIRE YOURSELF TO WIN

This nugget encourages you to inspire yourself to the top. Inspire yourself; motivate your world! No one will make you to be passionate in chasing your dreams. No one will make you better if you have not decided to become a better you. People can motivate you to get things done but they will not do the work for you. The power to achieve is deposited in you. You are the only one who has the power to inspire yourself. Nothing extraordinary will happen until you get passionate to change your world. This truth stands out anywhere in the world.

## NUGGET FIVE: DRESS UP AND SHOW UP!

The fifth nugget tells the reader to step out and make

things happen. Get ready! Step out with a winning mindset. Face your fears! You must defeat your fears to conquer your world. You must take the leap of faith. Nothing great comes easily. Success requires work and faith. You must work and have faith in your dreams. Follow the noble path that leads to success. You must pay the price that will take you to the top. Getting to the top is not easy. Staying at the top is not easy also. Everything about real success requires consistent and strategic efforts.

## NUGGET SIX: YOU CAN DO IT!

The last nugget in this book encourages you to take your dreams, talents, skills and all you got to the marketplace. This is where you get value. Don't sit and do nothing. Take what you got to the *stage* and create value. Create the world you desire! You are expected to develop the attitude of a winner. You are expected to wake up daily believing you can do it. You must believe you can achieve your goals. Once you think it, you must agree with the inner-you and do your best to make it happen. This is the first motivation you give yourself. Remember, thinking is not enough; you must think, believe and act. It is when you follow this sequence that you achieve your dreams.

*We cannot become what we need by remaining*

# FIRST THINGS FIRST

*Remember your focus determines your reality.*
**George Lucas.**

*what we are.* – John C. Maxwell.

Successful life follows a defined order. The man on a journey must define how he will embark on the journey. He does the first things first. He designs the way to go and how to get there.

Every airplane takes off from an airport. Every great work begins with a good plan. Doing the right things at the right time is the way of successful people. You must be orderly. You must do first things first if you truly want to be successful. Success doesn't happen by accident. Successful life is planned for. You plan and work for it.

Folks who succeed in life are individuals who do things that attract success. Everyone have the right to be successful. No one has exclusive right to success.

We all have equal right when it comes to accessing a successful life. But the challenge most times is that a lot of people start and continue the journey of life the wrong way. These sets of people begin life from a wrong footing and continue that way without changing their ways. Where you began your life is not your fault but the place you will end is totally your making. The place you were born is not your making, but the height you will attain in life is in your hands.

A lot of people dream of beautiful life. They want to have everything they wish for in their lives. But the irony is that many people lack the staying power to fight on in life in order to achieve the beautiful world they desire. Folks just sit down and dream of good things of life without making efforts to achieve them. Life doesn't work that way. What you give to life is what you will get in return. You are called to give the best to life in order to receive the best from life. This is the way it works. The first thing to do is to be organized. Try to organize yourself before you set out. Design a plan for yourself. Determine how to achieve your plan, and do your best to make your dreams come true. You must get to work!

## THE POWER OF VISION

Roman Philosopher, Seneca once said, "*To the person who does not know where he wants to go there is no favorable wind.*" To the man who has a vision, everything is possible. To the man who has no vision, everything is impossible!



Success or failure in life is deliberate design. You have what it takes to determine the path to follow. You are the chief driver of your journey. You need to do your best and believe in God to make your dreams come to reality. I believe in The God Factor. I also believe in the You Factor. You need God who gives divine ideas. You need you to work your way to the top. This is the secret to success. This is my winning strategy. A lot of successful people follow this path. Try it.



To inspire yourself in life, you should first design a path for yourself. You should know where to begin, when to begin, how to begin and the means to sustain your journey in life. You must set a personal vision. The vision you set for yourself gives your life a defined direction. Your vision is your reality.

Personal Vision influences all areas of your life - including spirituality, family, physical well-being, social world, leisure, and work. A comprehensible personal vision is a combination of your interests, abilities, personality, values, goals, experience and family. This is why I maintain that setting vision for yourself and following the path is a diligent work. The good news is that setting personal vision and following through lead to a successful life. The bad news is that many folks have not defined the path to follow in life. This is why I encourage you to read this book and implement the recommendations herein.

I have studied the lives of some successful people and have come to a conclusion that these folks make deliberate efforts to inspire themselves to success. They design a path that lead to success and follow that path diligently. Determining personal vision is imperative to what you will become - because it tells where you want to be. As explained earlier, the concept of vision is not as simple as it appears but it is the core of your existence. The vision you designed for yourself is your reason for existence. It defines why you do the things you do. It gives your life a meaning and the right direction.

A battle ready army commander prepares his war plan before setting out to the battlefield. No brilliant commander will go to war without a plan. The plan defines the battle. The plan determines how the battle will be executed. This is how it happens in life. Life is a battlefield and only folks who have defined their paths will win the battle.

The place of vision, plan and work are irreplaceable in the ladder of success. Before a captain of a ship begins a sail, he must first determine his destination, and how to navigate the path that will lead to his destination. You must plan how to succeed in life. Success is a deliberate design.



A traveler without a destination will end up in the Wonderland! Successful people decide their destinations before setting out for a journey. This is the way of the wise. You are called for a purpose. Identify your purpose and begin now to add value to your world. You are not one of the numbers. You are unique; you are special. You have a unique mission to accomplish in life. Discover this mission and be happy in life. Live a life of Vision. Live a life of Goals and Principles. Follow a defined path in life. This is how to create the world of your dreams. Go and make a difference.

## YOUR MISSION IS VITAL

Achieving success in life is work in progress. It is a long journey. You need to continue doing your best and your best must be good enough. You need to determine your mission. Your mission talks about what you do today that will help you achieve your vision. While your vision is in the future, your mission is immediate. Your mission is that path that will take you to your vision. They are the things you do today that will make you achieve your vision. What are you doing at the moment? Have you sharpened the axe? Are you doing the right preparations? How are you tilling the ground? Do you have the relevant sills that will make you stand out in your world? Are you mingling with the right circle? How innovative are you? Are you getting better by the day? You must provide answers for these questions. This is the beginning part. This is the right way to design a mission that will lead you through.

If you know where you are going, any road will lead you there. If you don't know where you are going, no road will lead you there. Vision tells you the "Where" and Mission tells you the "How." Without identifying your destination, the journey won't commence. The "How" [mission] is unnecessary if there is no "Where" [vision.] The concept of vision and mission is a core message of this book - because it is the foundation upon which every other thing stands.



As explained earlier, your vision is the destination you want to arrive at, and your mission is the things you do that will take you to that destination. While vision is a metal image of your destination, mission is the vehicle that takes you to that destination. You need these two in the journey of life.

Your mission determines what you will achieve. The things you do today will determine the results you will get tomorrow. Your today's work is your tomorrow's reward.

Setting and achieving goals is a function of the work you put in the project. This book, *Be Inspired* is not just a book that will awaken the giant in you. It will also encourage you to till the ground. I believe that the right efforts invested in the right place will yield the right results. This is my philosophy.

*There are three steps I discovered in setting and attaining your purpose in life, which are:*

[1]  **Identify your Vision and define a Mission:** It takes a purpose before a direction. When you know where you are going, every road will lead you there. When you don't know where you are going, no road will lead you there. This is my regular thought. Set clear vision; the one that is so apparent that you can "see" and "touch" with your hands. When you do this, the next stage is to design the way to achieve what you planned for yourself. This is how to live a life of purpose.

You must determine the way to reach your destination. This is the time to decide if you are going by airplane, ship or bus; but in all, you must follow a path that will lead you to your destination. Your main goal is to reach your destination. It is your duty to choose the appropriate means that will convey you to your destination.

Your mission defines the pathway you will follow daily. It tells you the work to do today. It tells you the right skills you need to acquire and the right preparation you need on the journey. Without vision, you start nothing. Without Mission, you achieve nothing!

[2.] **Believe in You:** It takes believing before achieving. It is natural to work hard in what you believe in. "Believ-ability" is "Work-ability." You have to believe in your abilities with your entire life. You must develop the right mindset. If you don't believe in yourself, no one will believe in you. Your vision and mission in life will suffer setbacks if you don't believe in them.

> *Without vision, you start nothing. Without Mission, you achieve nothing!*

As a Sales Trainer, I teach salesmen to sell the product to themselves first before they sell to the prospect or customer. You need to buy the product in your mind before you sell it to your prospect or customer. You cannot give what you don't have. The works of your hand will be successful if you keep believing that you will be successful and keep doing the right things that will attract the success you desire. You attract what you wish and work for.

[3] **Take the First Step:** When you have set the vision and determined the mission and believed in the path you designed for yourself, the next step is to make a move. Take action! You don't set a vision and go to sleep. You must make it happen by taking the right step.

It takes the first step to begin a Journey of 1,000 kilometers. That first step is vital. You must take the first step; you must take off - if you must attain your goals. You must wake up from sleep if you want your dreams to come true. You must set out to do the work aspects of realizing your vision. It takes a fight before a Champion. Every champion is declared after winning a fight. It is your duty to announce your arrival to your world by being outstanding in your work; by making a difference. Let your presence be felt. People celebrate actions not thoughts. Take the first step now and achieve your goals.

## INVOKING THE REAL YOU

Before you begin the journey to the *land of success -* which I believe is a long expedition; you must sit down and discover the person who resides inside. The real you is within. The real you is serene and equipped to do great things only if you discover what you have. The real you do not emerge in a noisy atmosphere; it comes out when it is called upon.

Just wait a minute as you read this part. Think deeply about yourself. Have you done that? Ask yourself why you are here; were you born to fill up a space? You need to ask yourself salient questions that will awaken the real you.

The real you only emerges in an environment it is needed. It doesn't come out everywhere. It comes out only where it will be valued and utilized. This means that you need to *feed* the things that will develop the man within.

You need to *nourish the inner-you with the right food.* The man within develops when you take in the right information. You need to determine the things you see, hear and do. You need to watch the circle you identify with. You need to be alert in the mind. These are the things that inspire the inner-man.

As a creative mind, I have grown in my career to conclude that there is an energy that comes from within. I call it Divine Ability. This strength comes from above and it is deposited within. This is The God Factor I talked about earlier. The Divine Ability that is deposited within cannot come out except you invoke it. You need to learn the way that leads to greatness. You need to know the way that enhances the work of God in your life. Always embrace the God Factor if you want to become an extraordinary individual. Successful people discover this success secret. You too can be next. Always do your best to be on the right path. Stand on a firm foundation and follow the right direction.

Doing first things first is the right way to inspire yourself. You cannot inspire yourself when you are standing on a wrong foundation. Decide today to do things differently. It takes this decision to get to the next level in life.

*Consequences are governed by principles, and behavior is*

# INSPIRING NUGGETS

*governed by values, therefore, value principles!*
– Stephen R. Covey,

1.  Every airplane takes off from an airport. Every great work begins with a good plan.

2.  Life is a battlefield and only folks who have defined their path will win the battle.

3.  The place of vision, plan and work are irreplaceable in the ladder of success.

4.  Vision tells you the "Where" and Mission tells you the "How." Without identifying your destination, the journey won't commence.

5.  It takes believing before achieving.

6.  You attract what you wish and work for.

7.  Let your presence be felt. People celebrate actions not thoughts. Take the first step now and achieve your goals.

*The more you prepare
to win, the more you
create chances to win.*

# SHARPEN THE AXE

*Give me six hours to chop down a tree and I will spend the first four sharpening the axe.*
**Abraham Lincoln**

---

*Do first things first, and second things not at all.*
- Peter Drucker

On 28th September, 2018, I went to Glendora Bookshop at Ikeja Shopping Mall to check some books. I got there and met a fine, brilliant and outstanding senior citizen who came to buy books. His name is Mr Bertrand Eneremadu. I liked the way he talked about books. In fact, he *celebrates* books! I didn't hide my feeling of approval when I noticed those qualities, and I moved to him and introduced myself. Mr Eneremadu is a good storyteller. He told us at the bookshop how he started acquiring books since 1964 and he has a lot of books in his library. Pointing at his bag, he said, "What I have in this bag are books. I read books when I am waiting at the airport or anywhere. I use books to utilize my idle time. I read a lot and I have imbibed this habit in my children." He expressed passionately how reading books helped to prepare him in life. I promised Mr Eneremadu that I will share my encounter with him in this book to tell how books can transform individuals. Francis Bacon rightly stated that reading maketh a full man.

Abraham Lincoln borrowed a lot of books to sharpen the axe. He had a humble beginning but that didn't discourage him from doing his best to change his story. It was recorded that the 16th US president had to trek for miles to borrow books. Abraham Lincoln sponsored himself to become a Lawyer and failed elections several times before winning the last attempt that made him the president. You must learn how to sharpen the axe. If you sharpen the axe; if you prepare better in life, you create better chances to win your battles.

*A blade that is not sharp doesn't cut down trees!*

How do you prepare yourself before setting out? Do you have a talent or skill? How have you been sharpening your skills or do you think you don't need to prepare before you get to the arena? Preparation is imperative to success. You are as good as the level of your preparation. A blade that is not sharp doesn't cut down trees!

I am a motivational speaker but my style of motivational speaking is embedded in doing the right things. I believe that when you do the right work and inspire yourself to succeed, you will succeed. I also believe that every good work comes with the right preparation. You are what you think and do. You cannot talk about what you do without talking about how you prepared before doing what you did. In fact, the more you sharpen the axe, the more you increase in knowledge and ability and the more you succeed. On the other hand, the less you prepare, the more you expose yourself to failure. My experience in life taught me this.

The concept of sharpening the axe is relevant in any life endeavour. If you want the axe to do more work, you need to sharpen it now. If you want to get more things done in life, you must begin now to develop yourself in the areas that will help you achieve your goals. There's no better counsel than this!

## CAREFULLY MAKE YOUR CHOICES

Jim Rohn once wrote, "*It doesn't matter which side of the fence you get off on sometimes. What matters most is getting off. You cannot make progress without making decisions.*" The choices you make are vital. Before you sharpen the axe, you must sit down and take decision about how to go about it. This is the time you choose the circle you keep. This is the time you take a decision on the path to follow. This is the time you ask yourself vital questions concerning the things you do and why you do them.

Life is full of hurdles. People who will triumph are

folks who took the right path. The right path is seen in the choices we make. Choices you make before beginning a journey can make or mar that expedition. It takes the right thinking and the right decision to arrive at the right actions; and the right actions lead to the right results. This sequence leads to success.



The major distinction between successful and average people is the choices they make. Successful people make necessary choices even when it is not convenient for them. Average people still go for the wrong choices even when they have a lot of options!

Make the right choices or the wrong choices will make you!

The world we live in today didn't provide a lot of good choices for folks. Wrong choices exist everywhere. You are definitely going to make a lot of mistakes when you go with the crowd. *Bandwagon Effect* has always been a problem. People follow others without reasons. They just follow! This is what I call *The Crowd Mentality*. Folks often follow the crowd. They go with what they think is popular even when what is assumed to be popular doesn't make a lot of sense. The unfortunate thing is that these crowds often stay on the wrong lane! This is the irony. This is why you must look before you leap.

Our world today provides very little options that will aid in making good choices. Look around you and observe the type of: Music, Value System, Standard of Education, and so on. The things you see around you are stuff that encourages wrong choices. Listen to the lyrics in some of the music you hear today. Sometimes I wonder where some musicians get their inspiration!

The challenges in our society today are broad. Our leaders have failed us too by not ensuring the right environment that will encourage the right values.

The future belongs to the few individuals who will decide today to see the world in another paradigm; the paradigm of emancipation of the mind and shifting from the status quo. The question is, "Are you among the people who will make the world a better place?" You have the answer.

## WHEN THE CHOICE IS FAULTY

The choices we make today determine what will be tomorrow. Good choices today result in better life tomorrow. Wrong choices cause a lot of damages; they determine wrong directions for the individuals who made them, and affect the society negatively. The things that will succeed or the ones that will fail start from the choices we choose, the decisions we make and the actions we take.

Let me take a little time to talk about why I recommend that you watch the choices you make before you set out in the journey. Investing time to decide on the choices to embark in life is imperative. You need to make choices concerning where and how you will spend your time. The circle you mingle with matter a lot. Friends fail people these days. It takes time to find one good friend. The circles you identify with contribute to a large extent what you will become. The wrong associations often time lead folks to the wrong lane.

Today's environment is facing challenges to uphold morals in the society. The value system has gone "crazy." Many folks celebrate emptiness nowadays. Many people get it wrong in our world today by chasing the wrong things. The order of the day is Quick Fix. A lot of people are in a hurry! This is the trend we see in our part of the world. This mentality has destroyed our value system. Young folks now want to make money even without working for it! What of our Standard of Education? That has gone terribly bad too. A lot of graduates cannot write one page proposal! Many students today want to score good grades in examination without reading their books. This is the situation we are in today.

Several quarters got its share of the systemic depreciation of values. Some businesses people want to make unjustifiable profits in business transactions. Some public servants go to work without thinking of how to add value in the system. Many politicians misappropriate funds as if the world is ending today. These are challenges facing our society today and this is experienced more in developing countries of the world. Too bad! This is where we found ourselves. But men of good conscience still live up to expectation in this near disappointing environment. They still make the right choices in the face of these happenings. They still do the right things.

Move on with the right attitude and take charge of the things around you. Be you. Allow the original you to emerge.

Don't waste your time following the crowd. Socrates once defined the wrong crowd as *Foolish Majority*. I agree with this because I have achieved a lot in Serenity. Be calm and always be at the right place, at the right time and doing the right thing. Withdraw yourself from the Noisy Crowd. Choose your environment and your crowd. Serenity begets inspiration. You need a lot of inspiration to be successful. Most ideas are created in a calm atmosphere. This is how to attract intuitive knowledge. What I am saying here may not be easy to comprehend - if you have not developed your mind-power. But the good news is that every positive attitude is learnable. Go get the things that will add value to your life. Decide to make the right choices today. Jonathan Winters says, "*If your ship doesn't come in, swim out to meet it.*" This is the mindset of champions. Go out now and make the right choices.

## PREPARING TO WIN

Benjamin Franklin once said "*An investment in knowledge pays the Best Interest.*"

The Bible records that Solomon was the wealthiest and wisest king because he prayed for something uncommon. When it was time for King Solomon to ask God for a favour, he asked for only one thing, Wisdom; he didn't ask for riches. Every good thing is embedded in wisdom. Wisdom is the correct application of knowledge.

The importance of wisdom and knowledge cannot be over emphasized. You need a lot of information to succeed in this challenging world. You can't Be Inspired without Information. Knowledge is Power. The more you acquire knowledge in your field, the more you excel in that area.

The man who is knowledgeable enough controls his world. We need the right knowledge to excel in our endeavours. Invest in knowledge. Go all out to acquire it. This doesn't come cheap but it's doable. Pay the price. Invest the energy and time required to increase from within. Nothing good it is said comes easy. Investment in knowledge is one of the best investments because you cannot earn beyond your capacity. Your income is a function of your know-how.

The logic of expansion is simple: If you want to expand, simply increase ability to perform. If you want to increase ability to perform, simply enhance knowledge. This has been my guiding principle on performance. You too can apply it.

In the course of my career, I developed steps that will help advance in knowledge and build capacity. These steps will help to equip the man or woman who wants to be inspired. They are:

1.  *Get Educated*: I see education as the basic foundation needed in the journey of life. Education is like the farmer who waters the ground before planting. If the ground is watered properly and is rich enough, the farmer will harvest bountifully. Education prepares the mind to take in and analyze information properly. The best gift you can give to an individual is to educate that person. When you do this, you have created the right foundation for the individual to take off.

2.  *Continuous Learning and Personal Development:* Learning is a constant process. The difference between education and learning in this context is that education has a defined period to conclude, but learning is nonstop; it is all the time. Learning is a lifelong project. Gaining admission into a secondary school or university requires that you graduate someday, this is education. But learning goes beyond this. Learning is when you do the things that will expand the man within. It could be by attending training programme, reading a book, listening to an audio learning programme, meeting an inspiring person who helps you to get better, getting a mentor, visiting an inspiring place, and so on. All these help to equip you to become a better person.

3.  *Get a Mentor:* One of the differences between successful people and average ones is the quest to

learn. Successful people seek knowledge everywhere and at all times. They make out time to learn. They go to places that will enrich their lives. They look out for new ideas. But this is not the case with average people. Average people think they know it all. Since they know everything, there is nothing new to learn and there is also no need to seek whom to learn from! This is the real example of where people plan to fail.

Since I learned the concept of seeking a mentor in core areas of my life, I have continued to increase in those areas. Getting a mentor is one of the easiest things to do in life. Yes, it is. You only need to identify the person and follow him up. Today's world is a global village. You can connect with someone in Africa, North America, Europe, Asia, etc, from the comfort of your phone. Distance is no longer a barrier. Get a mentor today!

There are lots of smart people who have passed through the path you are trying to begin. It's smart to find out from them the way they did it. This will make your expedition easier and faster. Read the stories of people you admire. Find out why they made it. Discover how they surmounted the obstacles that came their ways. This is a smart way to succeed.

4.  *Sharpen Your Skill:* Do you have a skill? What can you do with your hands? It's time to sharpen your skills. It's time to do something with your hands.

Get busy.

The challenge we have in the business world today is not necessarily unemployment. The main issue is short supply of the right skills. People who have the right skills to get things done are in short supply! We once got recruitment assignment from a company to employ and train outstanding sales professionals. It took us time to get the right candidates for the job. There are lots of people in the marketplace but the challenge is getting the right ones that are qualified to do the job. This is where sharpening your skills comes in. Try to learn something new. Get a new knowledge that will make you standout in your industry. People look out for folks that will bring value to the table. Nobody goes to the negotiation table empty-handed. You must come with value to take value from the negotiation table. Do everything you can to get better. Work on your talent. Don't just sit down and celebrate your talent without doing something to make it better. Your talent should standout. Champions don't hide in the crowd. Learn something today that will make you an outstanding individual.

> *You must come with value to take value from the negotiation table.*

Never see quest for knowledge as an expense, rather see it as an investment. This is the mindset of successful people. Folks find it difficult to

search for new information when they see it as
expenses. Seek to improve everyday in your area
of calling. You grow when you seek knowledge.
You lose nothing when you follow this path.
Trust me on this. Remember the maxim, "*If you
say Education is expensive, try ignorance.*"

*Before anything else, preparation is key to success.*
– Alexander Graham Bell

# INSPIRING NUGGETS

1. You are as good as the level of your preparation.

2. You are what you think and do.

3. Life is full of hurdles. People who will triumph are folks who took the right path.

4. The major distinction between successful and average people is the choices they make.

5. The choices we make today determine what will be tomorrow. Good choices today result in better life tomorrow.

6. Be calm and always be at the right place, at the right time and doing the right thing.

7. The logic of expansion is simple: If you want to expand, simply increase ability to perform. If you want to increase ability to perform, simply enhance knowledge.

*The pathway to your destination may be thorny, but you determine the pace.*

# YOU DETERMINE THE DIRECTION

*I can't change the direction of the wind, but I can adjust my sail to reach my destination.*
**– Jimmy Dean**

———  ❧  ———

*By failing to prepare, you are preparing to fail.*
- Benjamin Franklin

You have great abilities more than you can imagine. The things you cannot achieve are the things you have not settled on. No matter how it may seem, no matter how tough it looks out there; it is your duty to determine the direction of things. "*Tough times never last but tough people do!*" Robert H. Schuller wrote this bestseller long time ago. You must keep moving on towards the right direction. It is your call to make your dreams come to reality.

Henry Ford once said, "*When everything seems to be going against you, remember the airplane takes off against the win, not with it.*" You have a lot of capacity within you. You can do a lot of things if you can take the first step. The first step is the most difficult step to take in a journey of a thousand kilometers. But that first step is imperative. It determines the direction of the journey. You must dare to take that first step.



Many dreams never saw the light of the day because the dreamers lacked the abilities to determine the right directions. They just got stuck on the way and allow their dreams to die! This is not good news. You must wake up if you want your dreams to come true. You must keep your dreams alive. You must work your way to the top. You must show self-leadership and belief in self. The way to the top is available for individuals who know exactly how to locate and use the ladder that will take them to the top. It is one thing to locate the ladder that will take you to the top; it is another to know how to use the ladder. Folks who will do well in the school of life are people who know these basic principles.

Keep your eyes on the ball. Giving up is not a smart option. If your dreams have gone obsolete; go back to sleep and come up with an innovative dream! In all, never lose focus on your direction; no matter how tough it may seem, keep moving forward towards the right direction that will take you to the top. Never give up.

## MY MENTOR'S ADVICE

My mentor Brian Tracy once counseled us in a seminar that successful people live life of goals and principles. This wise counsel from this global authority has helped me a lot in life. In order to ensure you are on the right direction, you must set clear Goals and determine guiding Principles. You need to set goals for yourself and go after them. You need to also determine Principles that will guide you in the journey. These two are vital in life. Your goals will tell you where you are going. Your principles will guide you towards the right direction. I have on many occasions done things because of my principles. I may not have gone for those lines of actions but on principles, I followed those paths.



No one stumbles on success. Real success follows a design. You need to follow the precepts that lead to success. You must be diligent in doing this. Goals and Principles give direction. They tell you where to go, when to go there, how to go there and what to do when you get there. A man or woman without goals and principles is simply living an unexamined life! Such a person will live life without direction. Socrates once said, "*An Unexamined life is not worth living.*" I totally align with this thought.

Many people fail because they didn't plan to succeed. On the other hand, the folks who are determined to

*You may not control the wind but you have all it takes to determine the direction of the sail.*

succeed go the miles required to get to the top even when a lot of folks kept mute without doing anything to change their situations. The difference is that the people who succeed decided to be successful in life. These sets of people may not have started well in the journey but they adjusted in the course of the journey. I often say that where you started the journey may not be your fault, but the place you will end is entirely your making. You may not control the wind but you have all it takes to determine the direction of the sail. You may not decide your place of birth but you have all it takes to determine your destination.

It is not a crime to fail. Failing is not entirely a negative thing. Failure is an integral part of success because in failing you learn something new. The thing that is not allowed in the ladder of success is to fail and stay down. Get up and keep moving! This is what living a life of principles will teach you. Successful people know this fact. When they fail, they get up and continue to move on - doing their best to get to the finishing line. They set clear goals that will give them direction. They develop the right character and attitudes that will lead them to the top.

The men who have planned to fail think differently because they didn't set goals that will spur them, they also didn't determine principles that will guide them. Because they didn't plan ahead of time, they wake up and live by the day. They just follow the programmes the day provides for them! This life style makes folks in this category to be reactive and not proactive. This makes them to see only the intricate part of every situation, develop negative attitude to life and give up without making efforts. Their negative attitudes never allow them to think differently. They just sit down and wonder how and why things happen even when things are going against them!

Set clear goals today and determine guiding principles that will lead you in the journey. This is the way to define the right direction for yourself. Principles will guide you during tough situations. Principles will help you to stay in the right direction no matter the pressure you are encountering. Goals on the other hand will make you to be consistent in following the paths you designed for yourself. Don't set out without these two. A journey that began well is half traveled.

## WHEN THE WIND THREATENS YOUR DIRECTION, KEEP MOVING!

On 23rd September 2018, Tiger Woods made his fans happy by winning 2018 PGA Tour Championship. Many had doubted if Woods would be competitive again but he proved naysayers wrong. Woods had many challenges in life. The evident of all was the celebrated divorce with his wife, which caused a serious nosedive in his career. Subsequently, he suffered several setbacks which affected his career adversely. But the exceptional golfer refused to give up. He refused to throw in the towel even when his rating was terribly low. He fought on to win 2018 PGA Tour Tournament! This winning was his first in five years!  Challenges of life will surely come. The wind of life will surely blow but the question is "Are you in charge?"

Vince Lombardi, American football player and coach, once said, "*It's not whether you get knocked down; it's whether you get up.*" It's natural for life to be tough. It's no news that folks are knocked down in the journey of life. We hear daily that people set out with beautiful plans only to fail along the line. Yes, this happens daily and they are no longer news. The main issue is what you did thereafter; how did you manage the situation to bounce back?

Life teaches us the good, the bad and the ugly. Sometimes you feel like throwing in the proverbial towel. You feel like quitting and leaving the struggle. No! Champions don't quit easily. They fight on until they win. Surrendering is not the solution. People celebrate success and not failure. It was reported that Nike released a new ad celebrating Tiger Woods Winning. Folks identify with success. Failure is an orphan. Fight your battles. Don't surrender to the wind of life. Be inspired by the crown you will win - when you are declared the winner. Get up again from where you fell. Pick up the remaining pieces and launch back! Yes, this is the way of successful people. When they are knocked down, they get up and fight back.

The man on the voyage will naturally experience ups and downs. The storm will naturally come up from time to time to threaten the journey but the man on the journey determines his direction. The visionary man on the expedition will continue the voyage in the raging storm. He moves on because he knows his direction and how to get there. He never allows the storm to take him to another direction. The storm rages, but the man on the mission controls the sail.

Get up and fight again. Believe you can. Believe you will win. Believe it's your turn to be celebrated. The loser is not the one who is knocked down. The main loser is the one who gets knocked down and stays down without fighting back to come up again. You have all it takes to bounce back. You are unstoppable! Get up and win your battles.

## MAINTAIN YOUR LANE

In following a defined direction for yourself, know that there is no competition in life. We all are running our different races, within our lanes and trying to get to our different destinations. Some are traveling 1,000 miles, some 500 miles, while others are going 300 miles, 200 miles, 100 miles, etc. Everyone is expected to complete his races in good time.

Your duty is to do your best in your lane and get to your destination happily.

You don't need to compete with anyone. Our destinations are not the same; neither is the path to our journey the same. We fight our individual battles. The ideal counsel is: Fight your battles and let me fight mine. We have distinct callings; let's do our stuff. We are all doing our individual stuff! Our individual assignments are led by our individual visions and our visions are powered by our mission.

You are only competing with yourself. Yes, you are your greatest competitor in this race. You compete with yourself daily to get better than the person you were yesterday. This is the Real Competition. This is the main Deal!



Continue your race. Maintain your lane. Be a better you and never be perturbed by distractions emanating from oppositions. Your main goal is to reach your destination. Your drive is to achieve your purpose. It is your duty to stay on course. It is your duty to be focused.

The challenge many people encounter most times is distractions that come from doing unrelated things. They get involved in tasks that are not within their lanes. These types of tasks will naturally lead to distractions. You must stay focused and follow your vision. Always remember your vision, mission and core values. These are the ingredients that will keep you focused in the journey of life.

Run your race with all the vigour in you. Always Say YES to Yourself. Let the YES you say to yourself be stronger than the NO coming from opposing parties.



Winning the race within your lane requires that you follow the right principles. Remember that the goals you set for yourself give you direction in all you do. Let them and be clear enough. Let the goals be big enough!

Keep flying. Set tall tasks for yourself. Don't be scared of targets. Champions set big goals and chase them daily. Let your dreams be gigantic! David had to bring down the big Goliath before he was anointed the king. The bigger the challenge, the bigger the reward. Face the fears you encounter in your lane and overcome them. There's no stopping you.  Define the path to your journey and take off. An identified route is half traveled. Believe you can do it. Let's get to the top together!

# INSPIRING NUGGETS

*Go confidently in the direction of your dreams, live the life you've imagined.* – Henry David Thoreau

1. You must wake up if you want your dreams to come true.

2. The way to the top is available for the individuals who know exactly how to locate and use the ladder that will take them to the top.

3. Keep your eyes on the ball. Giving up is not a smart option. If your dreams have gone obsolete; go back to sleep and come up with an innovative dream!

4. No one stumbles on success. Real success follows a design. You need to follow the precepts that lead to success. You must be diligent in doing this.

5. A man or woman without goals and principles is simply living an unexamined life! Such a person will live life without direction.

6. The thing that is not allowed in the ladder of success is to fail and stay down. Get up and keep moving!

7. Challenges of life will surely come. The wind of life will surely blow but the question is "Are you in charge?"

*The Power to Win is within You. You only need to Believe and Act!*

# INSPIRE YOURSELF TO WIN!

*If you can dream it, you can do it.*
**Walt Disney**

---

*Sometimes the smallest step in the right direction ends up being the biggest step of your life.* - Emma Stone

The Champion's Pledge.

I am a Champion!

I will do the right things daily to continue to be a Champion. I may fail sometimes but I will keep making efforts without giving up. I will show up daily. I will pray and believe in God. I will continue to study to get better. I will prepare to overcome my challenges. I will continue to love wisdom and seek knowledge. I will move with eagles. I believe that iron sharpens iron. I will not waste priceless time in places that will not add value because I understand that time waits for nobody. I believe in myself. I believe in my dreams. I will get into the ring and fight the good fight.

I believe I will win my battles. I believe I will reach my goals. I believe I will make a difference. Though it is not easy but I will fight on until I win. I pledge to be a better me daily. This is my pledge, so help me God.

What is your pledge? The best motivation is the one you give to yourself. Positive self talks beget inspiration. Make a daily inspiring pledge that spurs you to win.

The road to success is tough. You need all the motivation you can get to reach your destination. Sometimes, skills are not enough. You need to support your skills with the right inspiration. You may have the ability to execute a project but lack the drive to get started. This is the problem many folks encounter. This is usually caused by fear. Fear kills dreams. But the good news is that you can overcome your fears. You can defeat your goliath. You can overcome your challenges. The easiest way to defeat fear is to practice daily pledge strategy to motivate yourself daily. Inspire yourself to win. When you practice this, every limitation steps aside.

Inspire yourself; motivate your world. No one will make you to be passionate in chasing your dreams. No one will make you better if you have not decided to become a better you. People can motivate you to get things done but they will not do the work for you. The power to achieve is deposited in you. You are the only one who has the power to inspire yourself. Nothing extraordinary will happen until you get passionate to change your world. This truth stands out anywhere in the world.

Get up now and inspire yourself. Arise and proclaim that you can do it. Let the world feel the fire burning in you. Be self-inspiring and passionate about your beliefs. Make things happen!

## YOU ARE THE MAIN INGREDIENT

You have a calling; you are like salt in the soup. Salt give taste to the soup. Cooking as an art is a good example where each constituent brings to bear its ability in order to achieve a defined purpose in the soup. The Vegetable Soup needs oil, water, meat, vegetable, etc, to do the cooking. All these ingredients are important to making of the soup, but salt must be present in the soup to give it taste. Everyone has his own purpose in the journey. Everyone is called for a reason. But some elements are more important than the others, just like the example of salt in the soup. The place of Salt in the soup is imperative. Without salt, the soup loses taste!

You have a calling - just like the ingredients in the soup. You have a space to occupy. You have a message for your world. You have a duty here. You have a gap to fill. You have a beautiful calling and only you can fulfill that calling. Some assignments are not transferable. Some battles must be fought personally. Only you have the abilities to announce your presence.

The soup will be tasteless without the contribution of

the salt; everyone is called to achieve a purpose and your calling will remain unattended to if you fail to identify the way to get things done.

The time is still right to get started. The right way to start is to take a journey of self-discovery to discover yourself. Have you truly discovered yourself? Do you know yourself? Who really are you? Commencing this great journey of life will be an issue until you answer these simple questions. You must discover who you are and the purpose you are called. This may appear simple but it is one of the hardest things in the world. Identifying your purpose in life is not an easy task but it is doable. You need to get into yourself and do soul-searching to get the right direction.

Take a decision to do this today because it's the starting point. Go to God in prayer and ask Him to show you the way. You need divine ideas. You need divine direction. Trust me, you can't do this alone. I failed when I tried to do it alone. My vision today is guided by divine ideas. You need God to lead the way for you. He never leads anyone astray.

Take a decision now to take your rightful place. Discover yourself and your calling. Nothing will happen until you take responsibility of your life. Nothing will change until you change the way you do things. Discover your purpose in life and let great things begin to happen in your life. Life is beautiful when you discover your calling and the role you are expected to play. Greatness requires a price. You must pay the price to win the prize. The time is always right to do the right thing. This is your time to get it right. Just do it!

## AIM FOR THE BEST

You don't grow by contraction. You develop by expansion. Aim for the best. Go for the highest result. Excellence is a virtue and only those who dare get desired result. People fail because they aim so low and strike; not necessarily because the aimed too high. Your performance is a function of the level of your expectation and input. The more you aim high and work hard to attain the top, the easier and faster you succeed. Great mind and author, George Bernard Shaw puts it this way, "*If you want to hit the mark, aim above the mark.*" This is one of the secrets of success. Successful people don't reduce their targets in order to attain results; instead, they raise their expectations, abilities and know-how in order to attain desired results. Don't settle for the least. You are called for Excellence. You are the best. You just have to prove your worth and make a difference.

> *The way to the top is not easy, it has never been easy; and it is not planning to be easy*

Set new standards for yourself every day. Increase your expectations; let your target touch the *sky*. Be inspired to do the near impossible. You are outstanding; you are created to do extra ordinary things. Quit the ordinary. Be Fantastically Extraordinary! Yes You Can! Move on. Go ahead.

Don't stop. Never give up. Kill your fears and Take Charge. The way to the top is not easy, it has never been easy; and it is not planning to be easy. But only the few individuals who dare to win will succeed. Prepare to go the extra mile. Real success is for those who are willing to travel the miles it will take to get to the top. You can do this. The time to start is NOW!

## WATCH YOUR THOUGHTS

In the New Thought philosophy, the *Law of Attraction* is the principle that by focusing on positive or negative thoughts, people can bring positive or negative experiences into their life. The Law of Attraction is about attracting the things you desire by developing a mindset that agrees with those things. This means that you must develop thought processes that are in agreement with the world you want to create. This book recommends that you run far away from negative thoughts. Negative thoughts are the route to negative actions which end in failure. Practice positive thinking that will attract a fulfilled life to you.

*If you want to build a castle, think about castles; don't think about mud houses!*

Therefore, if you desire to launch aviation business, you need to visit the airport always and imagine yourself owning one. You need to study the ways to operate Airline Company. You need to know the technical requirements in the industry. You need to know how to go about the funding of the business.

You need to know a lot of people who know about aviation business.

If you want to build a castle, think about castles; don't think about mud houses! Think about owning some of those castles in New York! If you want to be successful, think, act and work like a successful person. "*If you want to be a millionaire, think like a millionaire,*" Bassey and Company's Television Series promoted this thought over 25 years ago. Positive thinking is a winning strategy.



You lose nothing when you engage your thought processes with great dreams. My counsel always is: Think Big and Act Big Also. When you imagine greatness, you should work hard to attain what you imagined for yourself.

As I have always maintained, achieving success in life is a function of your Thinking and Doing Abilities. Don't just sit at the comfort of your home and be wishing the things you want to happen. Wishful thinking doesn't make champions. Champions take action immediately! Action is what makes the difference. You must wish it and work it out. Success does not come by imagination alone. No one receives success on a platter. Success is earned and not served! The only place where success comes before work is in the dictionary.

Watch the thoughts you accommodate in your mind because they will turn to choices, decision and actions in the course of time. The actions you take will determine what you will become. Watch your thoughts. Be alert in the mind. Be self-responsible in order to inspire yourself to be successful. Everyone is fighting his or her own battle. Battles are won or lost in the mind. Decide today to win your battles in the mind before going to the battlefield. Everything is Possible if only you believe.

# INSPIRING NUGGETS

*What lies behind us and what lies before us are tiny matters compared to what lies within us."*
– Ralph Waldo Emerson

1.  The best motivation is the one you give to yourself. Positive self talks beget inspiration.

2.  Sometimes, skills are not enough. You need to support your skills with the right motivation.

3.  Nothing extraordinary will happen until you get passionate to change your world.

4.  You have a space to occupy. You have a message for your world. You have a duty here. You have a gap to fill. You have a beautiful calling and only you can fulfill that calling.

5.  Greatness requires a price. You must pay the price to win the prize. Never give up.

6.  You don't grow by contraction. You develop by expansion. Aim for the best. Go for the highest result.

7.  The more you aim high and work hard to attain

*Without Thinking, You
Start Nothing. Without
Passion, You Drive Nothing.
Without Action,
You Achieve Nothing.*

# DRESS UP AND SHOW UP!



the top, the easier and faster you succeed.

*Life has no limitations, except the ones you make.*
— Les Brown

Four months before our wedding, Maureen and I travelled to Owerri, Imo State - Nigeria, my home town, to inform my father, Nze Chief F.O Emetuche that our wedding plans was on. We went to inform him about the date of the wedding and to seek his blessing. In the usual way I played with him, I asked jokingly if he was going to make it to the event because of his ill health. I told him that I don't want him to be sick on my wedding day. My 85 years old father smiled and got up from his chair to prove to me that he was strong. He danced happily round the sitting room and said to us, "My children, no matter what the illness does, I will dress up in my beautiful chieftaincy dress and show up to your wedding!" That was a great positive self-talk for a man who later passed on two months later. Though he didn't attend the wedding; he was positive even in sickness. You must profess optimistically; you must be positive no matter the condition.



The school of life teaches that if you don't show up in your case, everything stands still! All your plans will not be attended to unless you take action. You must dress up and show up! The beautiful life you desired for yourself will not happen if you don't step out and create it.

A lot of folks sit at home and wish to have a lot of things around them. They do nothing and expect a lot. Life doesn't work that way! Life is a *serious business.*



Life will give to you what you gave to it. The more you give life valuable things, the more life will respond by multiplying the valuable things and returning them to you in many folds. This is why you need to believe in yourself and in your dreams. This is why you need to do your best all the time. This is why you must step out and get your hands busy. This is the mindset needed to conquer your world. You cannot conquer your environment if you never dared. Step out and make a difference.

Educator and Author, Genevieve Rhode once said, "*No matter how you feel, Get Up, Dress Up, Show Up and Never Give Up.*" Yes, this is the way of self-starters. Giving up is never an ideal solution. Always remind yourself that it is your responsibility to achieve your goals. It is your responsibility to take yourself to the next level in life. Don't assume you will achieve desired results when you fail to do something. Life rewards hard working people. Life gives back to those who have the audacity to show up - to display their competence. It is when you dress up and show up that you connect to the right environment. The right environment cannot meet you; you step out to reach out to it. You step out to create the world of your dreams. If you don't venture, you will not achieve; you must take calculated risk to achieve your purpose in life. You must face your challenges squarely. You do this only when you show up and face your challenges. So, wake up from your slumber and believe you have all it takes to achieve what you planned for yourself. The world is waiting for your arrival!

> *Every priceless resource is hidden for the miner to discover it.*

## IF YOU WANT GOLD, THEN DIG!

Every priceless resource is hidden for the miner to discover it. The gold miner is expected to keep digging until he gets the gold. The process of digging is not easy but joy comes when the gold is discovered. Success annuls the toils that come with the digging. The pregnant woman forgets all the pains once she hears the cry of her baby. An atmosphere of achievement begets joy. Stay on the track and keep moving towards your goals. Keep digging. Keep believing. The gold is not far away from you. The next dig might be the long awaited discovery. The gold miner is always positive minded. He is hopeful that his efforts will yield good result.



You are like the miner. You are the one who will discover the gold you are looking for. You just have to hang on  on the right path and continue digging. You must continue to dig until you reach your goals. If you give up on the way, you waste your previous efforts. Pursue your goals with all you got.

You are as good as your last performance. This is what we were taught in the media world. You must keep doing the right things until it is confirmed that it is over. Champions don't quit in the middle of the game. Champions hang on and fight on until the last whistle. You are not judged by where you are coming from. You are appraised by where you are at the moment and where you are heading. You must ensure that you hang on; doing the right things, working hard and believing you will sail through the storms of life - no matter the situation.

Winston Churchill once said, "*If you are passing through hell, keep going.*" Hell in this context represents tough times and challenging situations. You must develop the right mindset to move ahead no matter the circumstance. Giving up has never been the best option. You must find a way to move on until your beautiful stories are told. Don't give up on the way because you are as good as your last performance. The person who endures to the end will reap the fruits of his labour.

Gold miners encounter challenges in their work. The miners sometimes risk their lives during the excavation. This is the hazard associated with the job. The miners will not give up in the middle of the job; they will keep doing their best until they achieve their goals. Gold miners would not discover gold if they sat at home without getting to work.

Get ready. Step out with a winning mindset. Face your fears! You must defeat your fears to conquer your world. You must take the leap of faith. Nothing great comes easily. Success requires work and faith. You must work and have faith in your dreams. Follow the noble path that leads to success. You must pay the price that will take you to the top. Getting to the top is not easy. Staying at the top is not easy also. Everything about real success requires consistent and strategic efforts.

Keep digging. Keep doing your best. Your wishes can come to life if you give them the necessary support. The time to start is now. Keep digging and keep discovering the gold.

## DEFEAT YOUR GOLIATH!

There is Goliath everywhere! Goliath, the giant comes in many forms, and can be seen in many places. The giant is in your workplace, in your business environment, in organizations and in everyday life. Goliath's main goal is to intimidate and conquer his victim.



Goliath in this context represents challenges and hurdles of life. You encounter Goliath any time you want to get to the next level in life. Success doesn't come easily. Successful life comes with a price. There's always a trial before a crown. These tests of life present themselves before you get to the next level. You will not make a move in life if you keep imagining the size of the obstacles standing on your way - without making attempt to overcome them.

I often tell people to prepare their minds to climb the staircase because the elevator is faulty! Don't pray that it gets easy. Pray that you have the capacity to overcome every obstacle that comes your way. You must develop this mindset. Prepare your mind to face any situation before getting to the arena. There are lots of challenges in the world today. Only folks who prepared their minds to face the good, the bad and the ugly will overcome in this demanding arena. You must defeat every Goliath in your life! You must climb every mountain standing on your way. You need to go over the mountain to reach the other side. The other side is where you get the good things of life but the giant won't let you have them without a fight! Goliath is the mountains of life you need to climb before reaching your destination. Once you conquer this mountain, you achieve your purpose in life.

You must overcome your Goliath to get to the next stage. It is your duty to discover this giant and the way to defeat him. You must devise your winning strategies. You don't go to war with a giant without a strategy. Your strategy must be unique. Your style should be strange to your oppressor. You are not expected to approach the giant with conventional weapons. You need to come with weapons that are strange to him. This was the strategy David used to defeat his Goliath. Coming to the battlefield with stones was astonishing to the giant but that was the real weapon of war! That was divine weapon that could penetrate his forehead.

In every Goliath, there is a David. In every Goliath, there is a weakness on the forehead! The open spot on the giant's forehead exposed him to attack. David discovered this weakness in the giant and the man went down without a fight. The little stone did the job! Of course this is God Factor at work. God has empowered us to discover the weakness in the Goliath of our lives. We cannot discover this weakness on our own. We discover it when we walk and work with our Creator, The Maker of Heaven and Earth. Divine abilities come from above. Uncommon winning strategies come from our Creator. This is why you need to connect with God in order to have access to uncommon ideas. This is the way of successful people. Men and Women who discovered this path are candidates for real success.

Every Goliath has one consistent feature. They are threatening by the day. The giant has the ability to put fear in you - in order to make you surrender to him. This was the case of David in the Biblical Story of David and Goliath. The giant bullied the people of Israel; he frightened them until David came into the picture. Don't expect your Goliath to go and sleep. Don't expect your Goliath to fizzle out. No! The giant is waiting for a big fight. Arise and defeat the giant!

Your Goliath will not let you be until you summon the courage to face him. You have all it takes to fight the battle. Go all out and win! Always remember that the gain of winning the giant is enormous. David was announced to the people of Israel after defeating Goliath. He got riches and also married the daughter of the king. Defeating Goliath brought David closer to the crown. This is the kind of reward you get when you get inside the ring and conquer your Goliath. Defeating the giant is a big achievement and the rewards are enough to motivate any man of faith to go to battle.

Start today to do those things that scare you. Stop running away from your challenges. Face them today and be celebrated like David. Remember, the bigger the battle, the bigger the reward.

# IF YOU ARE READY, HELPERS WILL EMERGE!

On 3rd October, 2018, I went to Centre for Management Development [CMD] to see the Acting Director General, Mr Bitrus Chinoko. CMD is a Federal Government Agency that certifies trainers and training companies. I had passed through certification programmes at CMD. So, I went there that fateful day to invite the DG to Nigeria Sales Conference. I got the idea to host the Sales Conference four years earlier but lacked the courage to launch it. The event will be massive and first open sales conference of that magnitude in Nigeria. Somehow, I felt I needed the right motivation. I had inspired myself that I can do it but I still wanted to get a push that would spur me to action. Sometimes, the *motivator* needs to be *motivated!* I motivate people to get things done, but this time, I felt I needed a motivating push to get things done.

Our company has built reasonable goodwill in our industry that will work in our favour - in hosting the conference. But something in me still wanted a push! This was my mood when I met the Director General. Accordingly, he read my letter and commended me for the idea to host the conference. He told me that the vision of Centre for Management Development is to build capacity in individuals and the agency will support me in this regard. He said, "I will attend the event with two Directors. We will give you every professional support." That was a great push for me!

Mr Chinoko's inspiring words gave me the needed audacity to intensify my efforts towards the event. When you are ready, helpers will emerge!

On December 8, 2018, we successfully hosted the first open Sales Conference in Nigeria with the theme: "The Salesman as Catalyst for Economic Development." Dr Leo Stan Ekeh, OFR, FNCS, Chairman, Zinox Group was the Keynote Speaker. Mazi Sam I. Ohuabunwa, OFR, FPSN, Founding President, Neimeth Pharmaceuticals Plc, President, Pharmaceutical Society of Nigeria, Dr Adebola Olubanjo, FCA, Chairman, Adebola Sobanjo Company, Soni Irabor, Chairman, Soni Irabor Media Group, Bitrus Chinoko, Acting DG, Centre For Management Development, Gloria Nwabuike, Head of Marketing, Nestle Waters, Biodu Ayeni, CEO, Affordable Cars Limited and Charles Iloegbunam, FNIMN, Chairman Asterisks Consults Limited, were worldclass speakers that spoke at the event. The conference recorded huge turnout. Salesmen and other professionals attended the event from different parts of the country. Once you can think it, and ready to work it; you can have it. The only place your ideas become impossible is in your mind. Believe that everything is possible. Give your dreams the wings to fly by doing the work that will make them come to reality.

In the journey of life, you must do your part if you truly desire success. Don't wait for anyone before you launch out. Start from where you are and keep moving forward towards the right direction. Don't wait for everything to be in place before taking your ideas to the marketplace. Start small and grow big. You are the main driver that will drive your dreams. You must take the lead in matters that concern you. Folks may not come to your aid if you have not commenced the journey. You must be seen to be making efforts every day. Help Agents will prefer to see how many miles you have traveled before coming to assist you in completing the remaining miles. They want to see what you have done for yourself before supporting you.

Helpers will come to you when they see that you are ready. You must help yourself before people converge to help you. You must agree with yourself before others agree with you. Help Agents will not locate you in your bed! They will locate you in the field.

I believe that the harder you work, the luckier you get. I am a promoter of this thought. Success locates people who are in the field working. Success will not locate the idle man's address. You must be found tilling the ground and working strategically towards your goals. Folks who will assist you to get to the next level in life will expect some efforts from you. They will expect to see you tilling the land before investing their seeds. This is a fair deal, I think. Keep doing your best.

We all know that a financial organization will not give out Loan except if the borrower contributes some percentage of the money he or she wanted, or if the borrower submits a kind of collateral before accessing the loan. It means that the borrower will make an Equity Contribution before the deal is done. The bank would want to know the amount you saved before giving you depositors' money. It is a win-win deal. No sane bank will give out loan if procedures are not followed. When this happens, then something is wrong somewhere.

The bank scenario applies to happenings in life. Most people will prefer to see you doing something meaningful before they will come to your aid. Folks want to sow on a fertile soil. Help Agents will prefer to assist people who are truly in need of assistance. It is easier for a brilliant indigent child to attract a help agent who will sponsor his or her education. It is easier for a hard working, talented and skilled fellow to attract grant for business than for an idle person to get such support. This is how it works in many places. Help Agents are more disposed to supporting people who truly need the right push. This may not be the case for an idle man who sits at home and does nothing; expecting Manna from above. Free Manna doesn't fall from above these days. You must work down your own manna!

You are expected to be at your best no matter the

# INSPIRING NUGGETS

situation. Be a person of value. People flock around a man or woman of value because that person gives value everywhere he goes.

*Thinking and Acting beget Success.*
**– George O. Emetuche.**

1.  You must dress up and show up! The beautiful life you desired for yourself will not happen if you don't step out and create it.

2.  Life rewards hard working people. Life gives back to those who have the audacity to show up - to display their competence.

3.  The right environment cannot meet you; you step out to reach out to it; you step out to create the world you desire.

4.  If you don't venture, you will not achieve. You must take calculated risk to achieve your purpose in life.

5.  Stay on the track and keep moving towards your goals. Keep digging. Keep believing. The gold is not far away from you. The next dig might be the long awaited discovery.

6.  You must overcome your Goliath to get to the next stage. It is your duty to discover this giant and the way to defeat him.

*Winners are not
people who watch and
wonder why things happen.
Winners are folks who get
up and make things
happen!*

# YOU CAN DO IT!

*The only person that can stop you is you!*
**George O. Emetuche.**

7.  Success will not locate the idle man's address. You must be found tilling the ground and working strategically towards your goals.

*Do you want to know who you are? Don't ask. Act! Action will delineate and define you.* – **Thomas Jefferson**

*Winning is an attitude of champions. You must fight your battles if you desire to win.*

**W**inners don't just wish for success; they go out and achieve it. You must develop the mindset of a winner if you truly want to win. You must think winning, you must believe you can win; you must work your way to becoming a winner. I agree with Les

Brown's thoughts when he said, "*It is not over until you win.*" Winning is an attitude of champions. You must fight your battles if you desire to win.

You are expected to develop the attitude of a winner. You are expected to wake up daily believing you can do it. You must believe you can achieve your goals. Once you think it, you must agree with the inner-you and do your best to make it happen. This is the first motivation you give yourself. Thinking is not enough; you must think, believe and act. It is when you follow this sequence that you achieve your dreams.

I once asked my mentor Brian Tracy a lot of questions about the journey of life. I wanted to define a clear direction for myself. I had a lot of things going on in my head that time. I wanted a guide and I reached Brian to advise me on the path to follow. He wrote me in this regard - where he guided me towards the right path.

In 2013 when Brian Tracy visited Nigeria on Seminar Tour, our company, The Selling Champion Consulting Limited was the sales and marketing organization that marketed the International Brand. I bought one of his books, SPEAK TO WIN a day before the seminar and gave him for autograph. Brian looked at me and smiled, and wrote in the book: "George, You Can Do It," and appended his signature. That singular motivation was a push for me. That gave answers to a lot of questions I was asking about my professional life. Yes, I can do it! In fact, I can now say, I am doing it! I am attaining my goals and setting new ones. I am overcoming my challenges. I am winning my battles. I am exceeding targets and setting new ones. I am developing new ideas. I am winning new markets. It has not been easy but we are on the right path and gradually getting to the destination. Yes, you can do it! You must develop positive attitude. You must inspire yourself to the top. That's one of the purposes of this book.

Your duty is to do your best all the time. You Can Do It, but doing it in this context is not by your making alone. You need the God Factor and The You Factor to have real success. You need God's help; you also need to help yourself. This is how to succeed in life. The God Factor is walking and working with God. This is my strength. This is the strategy I have applied overtime. It works. A lot of successful people follow this path because it never fails. I recommend that you try it now. When you identify the place of God in your life, He does the unimaginable things for you. You need divine ideas. You need divine grace. You surely need God's favour in this race. You are not a superman. Walk with God and be an outstanding individual!

Life provides you a lot of options and you are expected to make choices from these options. You have the right to choose the path that will lead to success. You also have the right to take the opposite direction. Either way you follow is a path that will lead somewhere. But the question is: are you following a path that will lead to fulfillment? You have the answer.

In all, remember that you owe yourself the duty to do all you can to succeed. Nobody will do this for you. Inspire yourself to win!

## YOU OWE YOURSELF SUCCESS

Mark Zuckerberg, founder of Facebook dropped out of Harvard to pursue his dream world; though he came back 12 years later to complete his degree at Harvard. In my opinion, dropping out of Harvard at that time was necessary because he needed to work fulltime to create the Facebook Brand. We all know the success story of Facebook.

I am a fan of Facebook because the social media platform was handy in promoting our company when we started. We explored the social network to promote our products and services. As at 3rd quarter of 2018, Facebook had 2.23 Billion monthly active users. This makes the American Corporation the biggest social network in the world.

I consistently follow the success story of the corporation till date. On 19th October, 2018, Facebook hired former British Deputy Prime Minister Nick Clegg to lead its global affairs and communications team. They now have the capacity to hire high profile individuals because the corporation has built a strong global brand. In 2018, Forbes rated Mark Zuckerberg the 5th Richest Man in the world.

This is truly a reward for hard work.

Today, nobody remembers that Zuckerberg dropped out of Harvard; everyone is talking about his success story. You must do your best to create your dream world. You owe yourself success. If your environment won't give you what you want in life, step out and create the world you desire! Mark Zuckerberg's story is a good case study.



No one celebrates intent. Folks celebrate achievements. If you want to be celebrated, you must convert your intents to actions. There's no short cut to success. The shortest path to success is thinking smartly and working hard. Intents without actions don't make champions!

What are you offering to your world? The clock is ticking! You must utilize the time you have appropriately. This is the time to give yourself and your world value. Time waits for no one. Time moves slowly and passes quickly. Are you still waiting or are you going to take the right action now? Are you going to launch out as the best product in the market or will you choose to remain a part in the crowd? Get your hands busy and make a difference! Get set to take yourself to the next level. You must develop the right thinking style. Great warriors win the battle before going to the battlefield. You must win from within.

Good products launch out immediately. You are like a

good product that has all the marketing support. This is the time to take your rightful place in the marketplace. You must take action to succeed in life. This is what you owe yourself. Inaction doesn't make champions. If you want to win a fight, you must get inside the ring and knock your opponent down. You must act now! You should think like the best all the time. This is a winning mindset. Never undervalue yourself. Inspire yourself from within. Never accept negative scripts from naysayers. Believe you can. You are not what you are. You are always what you think you are. The way you think and act make the difference.

Robert H. Schuller once said, "*The only place where your dream becomes impossible is in your own thinking.*" This can't be Truer.  Our actions follow our thought processes. The way you think is the way you act. You should know this fact and work with it too. If you see yourself as the best, then you are the best. If you see yourself as the weakest, then that posture becomes your reality. This is the way our world is programmed. You determine your story. You determine your script. Never allow the pencil in the hands of opposing forces. Write your story!

Onlookers could have different stories about you. This posture does not determine how you will end your story. Your destiny is in your hands. You have the power to determine what you will become. Your duty is to keep thinking the right things and keep working hard. The right thinking and the right work lead to success. Always follow the path of honour.

# SERENITY BEGETS INSPIRATION

Ideas rule the world. The more unique ideas you discover and execute, the more successful you become. Great minds are inventors. They create the right ambiance that will bring the next great idea.

As a creative mind, I have practiced this style for a reasonable time. Since I discovered that the more outstanding ideas I come up with, the more I distinguish myself from the crowd; I always create conducive atmosphere that will enable me achieve my goals. You need to learn how to create the right setting that will bring about the inspiration that will make things happen.

Achieving your goals in life comes with great character and attitudes. You must know the things to do and when to do them. This is the distinction between successful people and average people. Successful people do the rights things at the right time. Average people give excuses all the time.

Success in life is planned for. You are expected to periodically withdraw from the noisy crowd and seek the inspiration that will drive you to the next level in life.

I once read about Stoic Philosophers in the course of a research work. These great minds often withdrew from their environment anytime they want to come up with new thoughts. The good thing about them is that they come out with great works after this tranquil experience. This may seem unusual but I know you achieve a lot when you follow this path. Silence is gold.



I have grown in my career to know that you don't achieve a lot when you move with the crowd. You don't achieve meaningful things in a noisy environment. Serenity begets inspiration.

Bill Gates once withdrew from Harvard only to launch out later with Microsoft. Mark Zuckerberg of Facebook we told his story had a similar story at Harvard. **Steve Jobs** of Apple Corporation also dropped out of college so he could **drop** in to the classes that looked more interesting. It was told that Reed College offered the best calligraphy course in the country. In those classes **Jobs** learned about serif and sans serif typefaces, something with no practical application to his life at the time. You will notice that these great inventors have similar stories. They withdrew from regular things to pursue things that seemed abnormal! They followed their passion in order to create the world they desire.

The question is, Why the withdrawal from University or College? Let me clarify here that Harvard is one of the best institutions in the world. In my rating, I see Harvard as the best. So my posture here about these great folks withdrawing from Harvard or anywhere else has nothing to do with the standard of the great institutions. Having made this clarification, I will now proceed.

Swiss Psychiatrist and Inventor, Carl Jung, once said, "*He who looks outside, dreams; he who looks inside, awakes.*" These great men may have looked inside. You have a lot of deposits within. Greatness emanates from within. When I teach Performance Efficiency and Success Psychology, I tell my audience to practice what I call: Deliberate Withdrawal and Deliberate Focus. These concepts separate successful people from average folks. The model teaches that you deliberately withdraw from "Unnecessary Public" when you want to achieve extraordinary results. It is when you do this Withdrawal that you will focus on the things you want to achieve. This is a success secret.

The challenge is that this Character Trait is not easy to come by. You must be disciplined and result oriented if you want to attain this level of self-awareness and self-efficacy. You must distinguish yourself from the crowd. You must understand who you really are. You must believe in yourself and in your abilities.

I have achieved a lot of tasks using this formula, I wrote my book, "EVERYTHING IS POSSIBLE" in two weeks. I also wrote the book you are reading now, "BE INSPIRED" in two weeks - by applying this Serenity Model. You too can. You can't achieve this if you are a "Follow-Follow" kind of person! You must be self-motivated. You must have a direction in life. You must believe in yourself. You must take charge of your journey. These responsibilities are not transferable. They are your call. Take charge of the driver's seat and navigate your journey towards your destination.

Let me quickly add that Serenity Model is not anti social or anti people. I have always talked and written about Maintaining a Balance in all that you do. Maintaining a Balance in life seeks to nullify the weakness you will encounter in applying Deliberate Withdrawal and Deliberate Focus Concepts. Here, you do the right things at the right time in order to maintain equilibrium. You are expected to work at the right time, give attention to the family when you are supposed to; give appropriate time to your spiritual and social lives and of course maintain a healthy living. This is how to achieve Real Success. Every facet of your life must be working.

Try not to be "Too Public." Crowd does not achieve extraordinary results. Great inventions are achieved by the few who withdrew from the crowd with the intention to do things differently. This thought may sound strange for average minds but great thinkers know what I am talking about.

Let me give you an assignment. Take a decision now to withdraw for 30 days from: unnecessary gathering, avoidable places and stay away from idle minded friends. Do this with the intention to focus on achieving a particular task. Follow through your plans and see what you will achieve in 30 days. This is practical. Try it now!

# YOU MUST GET TO THE MARKETPLACE!

My village has a Local Market known as Eke Obi. The market is significant because villagers look forward to visiting the market every Eke Market Day for buying and selling activities. Igbo Calendar has four market days: Eke, Orie, Afor and Nkwo.  Igbo communities trade on different market days and ours is Eke which is the first market day. I remember those days how my father talked about the market and I admired how villagers came to the market with their fresh farm produce. Villagers that sell one thing or the other look forward to visiting Eke Obi Market Day because they sell greatly when their products reach the market.

This is the way it is in real life; this is the way it is in the business world. Every trader does his best to ensure that his products and services reach the marketplace. You must take your product to the market if you want to succeed as a businessperson. Your products or services won't be noticed until you get them to the business arena where buyers come to buy.

As a sales expert, I know that the aim of every company is to ensure that their product win its rightful share in the market. This is why company hires and trains salesman who will get things done. The marketplace waits for nobody. The people who will win in the market are the ones who are prepared to win. They are the people

*You must be willing to take your products to the market in order to sell them. Nobody will notice your product until you take*

who come to the arena with the right products and doing the right things. They are the people who are willing to go to the market in the first place. You must be willing to take your products to the market in order to sell them. Nobody will notice your product until you take it to the market.

You must be willing to launch your ideas. Your ideas will become mere fantasy if you don't take action to launch them out. What are you selling? What are you offering to your world? Everybody has something of value to offer. It is your duty to discover what you are called to offer. This discovery must be made by you. Nobody will do this for you. You must discover the products you are called to sell.

You have enormous deposits inside you, but you need to let them out. You need to conquer your world. Stop wondering why things happen. Get in and make things happen!

This is the time to rise up. This is the time to wake up from sleep. This is the time to execute the ideas you have been procrastinating. The people who will be celebrated are the ones who have the courage to move on - to tell their stories. Remember, nobody celebrates intents. This is the time to act. This is the time to make a difference. Inspire yourself to win. Be Inspired!

# INSPIRING NUGGETS

*Start where you are. Use what you have. Do what you can.*
**– Arthur Ashe.**

1   Winners don't just wish for success; they go out and achieve it.

2   Once you think it, you must agree with the inner-you and do your best to make it happen.

3   Yes, you can do it! You must develop positive attitude. You must inspire yourself to the top.

4   In all, remember that you owe yourself the duty to do all you can to succeed. Nobody will do this for you. Inspire yourself to win!

5   No one celebrates intent. Folks celebrate achievements. If you want to be celebrated, you must convert your intents to actions.

6   If you want to win a fight, you must get inside the ring and knock your opponent down. You must act now!

# OTHER BOOKS BY GEORGE O. EMETUCHE

THE SELLING CHAMPION

THE 11 IRREFUTABLE PRINCIPLES OF SUCCESS

EVERYTHING IS POSSIBLE!

THE 25 UNBREAKABLE LAWS OF SALES

THE ART OF SELLING

SUCCEEDING WITH YOUR SPOUSE

**FOR SALES TRAINING OR BULK
PURCHASE OF OUR BOOKS OR CDS,
PLEASE CONTACT:**

THE SELLING CHAMPION CONSULTING
LIMITED:
sales@thesellingchampionconsulting.com

Or Visit:
www.thesellingchampionconsulting.com
www.nigeriasalesconference.com

Or Call:
08186083133, 07060559429

www.ingramcontent.com/pod-product-compliance
Lightning Source LLC
Chambersburg PA
CBHW061249140726
47998CB00006B/2167